A Bunch of Punctuation

Poems selected by
LEE BENNETT HOPKINS

Illustrated by
SERGE BLOCH

WORDSONG

AN IMPRINT OF HIGHLIGHTS

Honesdale, Pennsylvania

TABLE OF CONTENTS

A Punctuation Tale   Rebecca Kai Dotlich   4

Comma   Lee Bennett Hopkins   6

Apostrophe   Amy Ludwig VanDerwater   8

The Dash   Charles Ghigna   10

. . .   Allan Wolf   12

Forgotten: A Colon's Complaint   Alice Schertle   14

!!!!!!!!—Superhero *Kaboom*—!!!!!!!!   Julie Larios   16

Stubby the Hyphen   J. Patrick Lewis   18

The Purpose of Parentheses   Michele Krueger   20

Period   Jane Yolen   22

Question Marks   Prince Redcloud   24

You Can Quote Us on That   Joan Bransfield Graham   26

Semicolon   Betsy Franco   28

Lines Written for You to Think About   30
(*Inspired by Carl Sandburg*)   Lee Bennett Hopkins

A PUNCTUATION TALE

Rebecca Kai Dotlich

Wake up!

An exclamation starts your day,
steers the way to a comma,
which brings you to pause
      in an inlet cove
         for a snack of shrimp,,,,,
then a mad dash sends you
swift and straight—like the *whoosh* of a sail—
into pockets of small waves;
here semicolon whispers
while sea's apostrophe tells a tale
of joining twenty-two ships or more
with a bridge called hyphen and
holding steadfast while waiting
through calm ellipses near the shore . . .
A colon is used to search the map:
North
South
East
West.
Which direction are we headed?
(Here come the parentheses—
it's the navigation test.)
Finally, you stop
on a sleepy spot.
You come to a small
period—a dot.

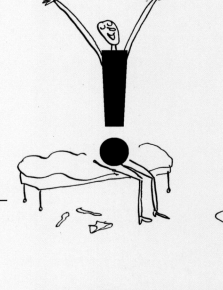

twenty two

Soon once again
you sail away
to the Island of *End of Day*,
where sky is a scribble
of lights and darks—

with
     "good night"

cuddled
in quotation marks.

"goodnight"

COMMA

Lee Bennett Hopkins

A comma
lets you stop,

pause,

enjoy the weather,

unlike a period,
which puts an end

to any
cloudy,
rainy,
snowy,
or sunny day,
at once,
immediately,

forever.

APOSTROPHE
Amy Ludwig VanDerwater

I'm flattered to be popular.
People love to use me.
But now I'll have to set you straight.
I hope that you'll excuse me.

I'm a sign of ownership
when I hang out with *s*.
If you see my sister's room,
you'll see my sister's mess.

I'm good at joining little words.
Could not changes to *couldn't*.
They are turns into *they're*.
Should not switches to *shouldn't*.

If you read and write, my friend,
it's your job to care
about me—small apostrophe—
for I work hard up there.

Use me to show possession.
Let me make contractions.
Don't just stick me anywhere—
or I'll create distractions.

they 're

a

shouldn

o

THE DASH
Charles Ghigna

A handsome mark,
understated,
the dashing dash—
underrated.

A subdued dude
in tweet and text,
he signals what
is coming next.

The daring dash—
an interruption—
is cause for pause,
a clear disruption.

A skip—a break—
a change of thought—
the dash is often
overwrought.

And so—he hangs—
a random rafter,
holding forth—
forever after.

. . .

Allan Wolf

The silent ellipsis . . .
replaces . . . words missed.
Three footprints . . . in quicksand.
A message . . . withdrawn.

The whispered ellipsis . . .
Three lunar eclipses . . .
When words fade to nothing . . .
They're going . . . they're gone . . .

FORGOTTEN: A COLON'S COMPLAINT

Alice Schertle

I wish to complain of the following:
neglect, disrespect, lack of use,
abandonment, utter exclusion.
I call it colon abuse.

SEE PAGE FORTY-THREE!

I'm hidden away in a textbook:
Punctuation Made Easy, no less.
Page forty-three is devoted to me,
but nobody reads it, I guess.

The comma, incredibly common,
butts right into line after line.
Couldn't there be a small place for me:
just one little sentence that's mine?

Use me to draw attention:
what follows is something of note!
Or I'll point to a list so nothing is missed:
umbrella, galoshes, and coat.

Even the semicolon
(that halfling) gets used now and then;
I can make what you write sound impressive and bright!
Please pardon the inquiry: *when?*

!!!!!!!!—SUPERHERO *KABOOM*—!!!!!!!!

Julie Larios

1 big *boom*!
2 *kapows*!!
3 in a row of wow, wow, wows!!!
4 *kahblooies*!!!!
5 *bops* and *bams*!!!!!
6 gee whizzes!!!!!!
7 *whops* and *whams*!!!!!!!
8 for the man, Super- or Bat-!!!!!!!!
9 for the woman, Wonder- or Cat-!!!!!!!!!
10 Someone help me—I CAN'T STOP!!!!!!!!!!
9 exclamation marks over the top!!!!!!!!!
8 great heroes, hear my call!!!!!!!!
7 for Spiderman climbing my wall!!!!!!!
6 for the green ones, Lantern and Hulk!!!!!!
5 for brains!!!!!
4 for bulk!!!!
3 stacks of comic books!!!
2 piles read!!
1 more *kaboom*, then it's off to bed!

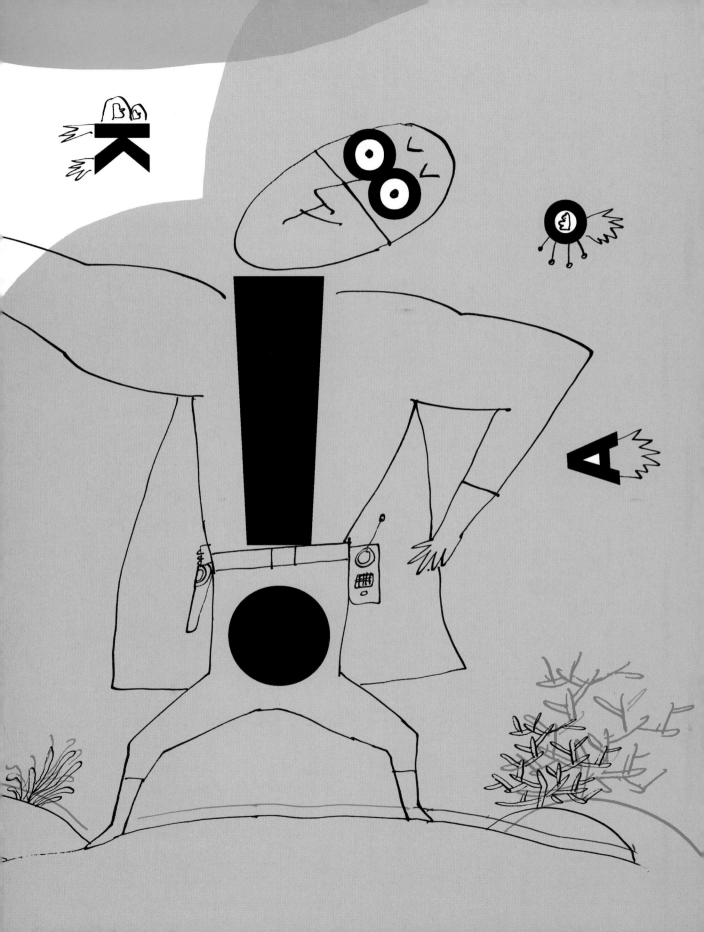

STUBBY THE HYPHEN

J. Patrick Lewis

Please don't confuse me with my cousin Dash,
Who interrupts your sentences. I am
That special link who knows just how to form
One nifty word in place of two. *Shazam!*

You may not notice me, but I'm a punc-
Tuation mark no one can do without:
A simple line between two words that can
Create cool wizardry with lots of clout,

Like *top-notch*, *five-star*, *president-elect*.
So pay attention when the grammar bird
Says *class* and *first* together to make *first-class*,
An honor that yours truly has conferred.

I'm one fine taste bud on the mother tongue,
Though readers are unlikely to applaud
Because I'm often seen but never heard,
A silent but fail-safe connecting rod.

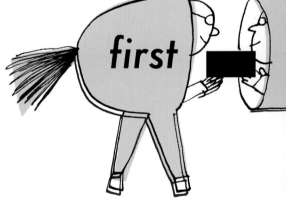

class

top ■ notch

five ■ star

THE PURPOSE OF PARENTHESES

Michele Krueger

inside a pair
( ) ( ) ( ) ( ) ( ) ( ) ( ) ( )
of slender curves

we'll hold your few
inserted words—

folded in
(without ado),
intended to
add meaning to

what you
want to say—

a brief aside
(a floating thought),

neatly lassoed,
grammatically caught!

(!) (!) (!) (!) (!) (!) (!) (!)

calf

COW COW COW

PERIOD
Jane Yolen

Period is the point that halts you:
small, black, hard at the end
of a sentence, a spot, a dot, a blot.

Tiny but certain, a final curtain.
You cannot go beyond it,
behind it, beneath it, over it.

You cannot roll through it.
You must wait on it, squint at it,
nod at it, shake your fist,
as if it were that eight-sided red sign
somewhere along a winding road
where you must come at last to a

      Full Stop

lest the Grammar Police get you.

Only then can you move on.

QUESTION MARKS
Prince Redcloud

Why?
Why?
Why?

Why
must
a question
always
be
followed
by
an answer?

Why?
Why?
Why?

Because!

Because?

Because!

YOU CAN QUOTE US ON THAT

Joan Bransfield Graham

"We travel
in pairs,
        we float
        in place,
a visual
tweak,
        to hug,
        embrace
the words
you speak.

We think
you're clever,
        witty,
        notable;
we aim
to make you
        highly
        quotable.

We'll spotlight
your words . . .
        create
        verbal sparks,"
said that
versatile duo—

Quotation Marks.

SEMICOLON

Betsy Franco

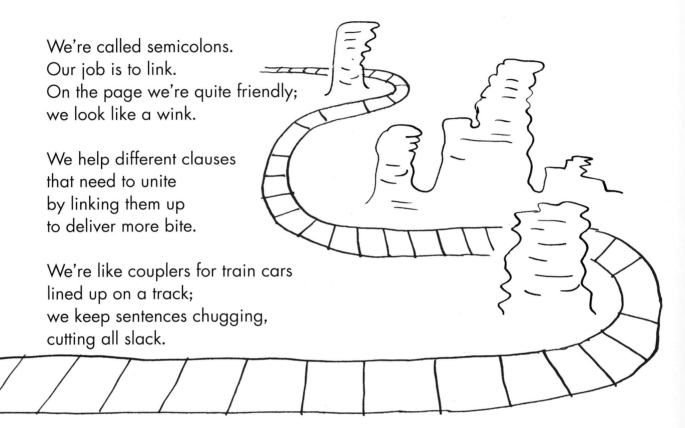

We're called semicolons.
Our job is to link.
On the page we're quite friendly;
we look like a wink.

We help different clauses
that need to unite
by linking them up
to deliver more bite.

We're like couplers for train cars
lined up on a track;
we keep sentences chugging,
cutting all slack.

LINES WRITTEN FOR YOU TO THINK ABOUT

(*Inspired by Carl Sandburg*)
Lee Bennett Hopkins

Can you write poems posing questions
    like who, what, where,
        when, how, and why?

Can you write poems using
    a series of commas with
    words like scented carnations,
    colorful columbine,
    creeping phlox . . .?

Can you write poems causing
    words such as:

    Whoopee!

        Whee!

          Wha-hoo!

    to look as if they are
    leaping off pages?

Can you write poems featuring
    an apostrophe, colon, dash,
    hyphen, question marks—
    even a couple of semicolons,
    bringing everything together
    with a period?

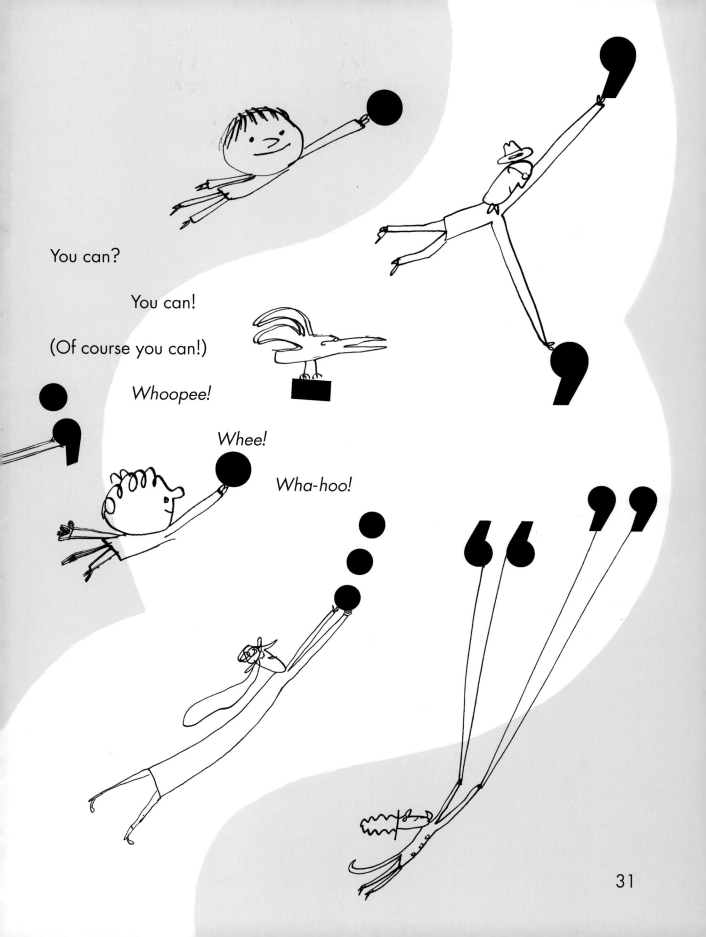

You can?

You can!

(Of course you can!)

Whoopee!

Whee!

Wha-hoo!

31

To Rebecca M. Davis—
who asked
so many **?????**'s
over twenty-five years
—and—
got me to answer
most of them!!!!!
—LBH

ACKNOWLEDGMENTS

Thanks are due to the following for use of works in this collection: Curtis Brown, Ltd., for "A Punctuation Tale" by Rebecca Kai Dotlich, copyright © 2018 by Rebecca Kai Dotlich; "Comma" and "Lines Written for You to Think About (Inspired by Carl Sandburg)" by Lee Bennett Hopkins, copyright © 2018 by Lee Bennett Hopkins; "Question Marks" by Prince Redcloud, copyright © 2018 by Prince Redcloud; "Apostrophe" by Amy Ludwig VanDerwater, copyright © 2018 by Amy Ludwig VanDerwater; and "Period" by Jane Yolen, copyright © 2018 by Jane Yolen. All used by permission of Curtis Brown, Ltd. All other works are used by permission of the respective authors, who control all rights; all copyright © 2018: "Semicolon" by Betsy Franco; "The Dash" by Charles Ghigna; "You Can Quote Us On That" by Joan Bransfield Graham; "The Purpose of Parentheses" by Michele Krueger; "!!!!!!!!—Superhero *Kaboom*—!!!!!!!!" by Julie Larios; "Stubby the Hyphen" by J. Patrick Lewis; "Forgotten: A Colon's Complaint" by Alice Schertle; and ". . ." by Allan Wolf.

The illustrator thanks Lisa, Mireille, and Sheina for their help.

WordSong
An Imprint of Highlights
815 Church Street
Honesdale, Pennsylvania 18431
wordsongpoetry.com
Printed in China

ISBN: 978-1-59078-994-0 (hardcover)
Library of Congress Control Number: 2017949852

First edition
10 9 8 7 6 5 4 3 2 1

Designed by Barbara Grzeslo
The text of this book is set in Futura and Neutraface.
The drawings are done in pen and ink and digitally colored.